How-To Guides for Fiendish Rulers

An Emperor's Guide

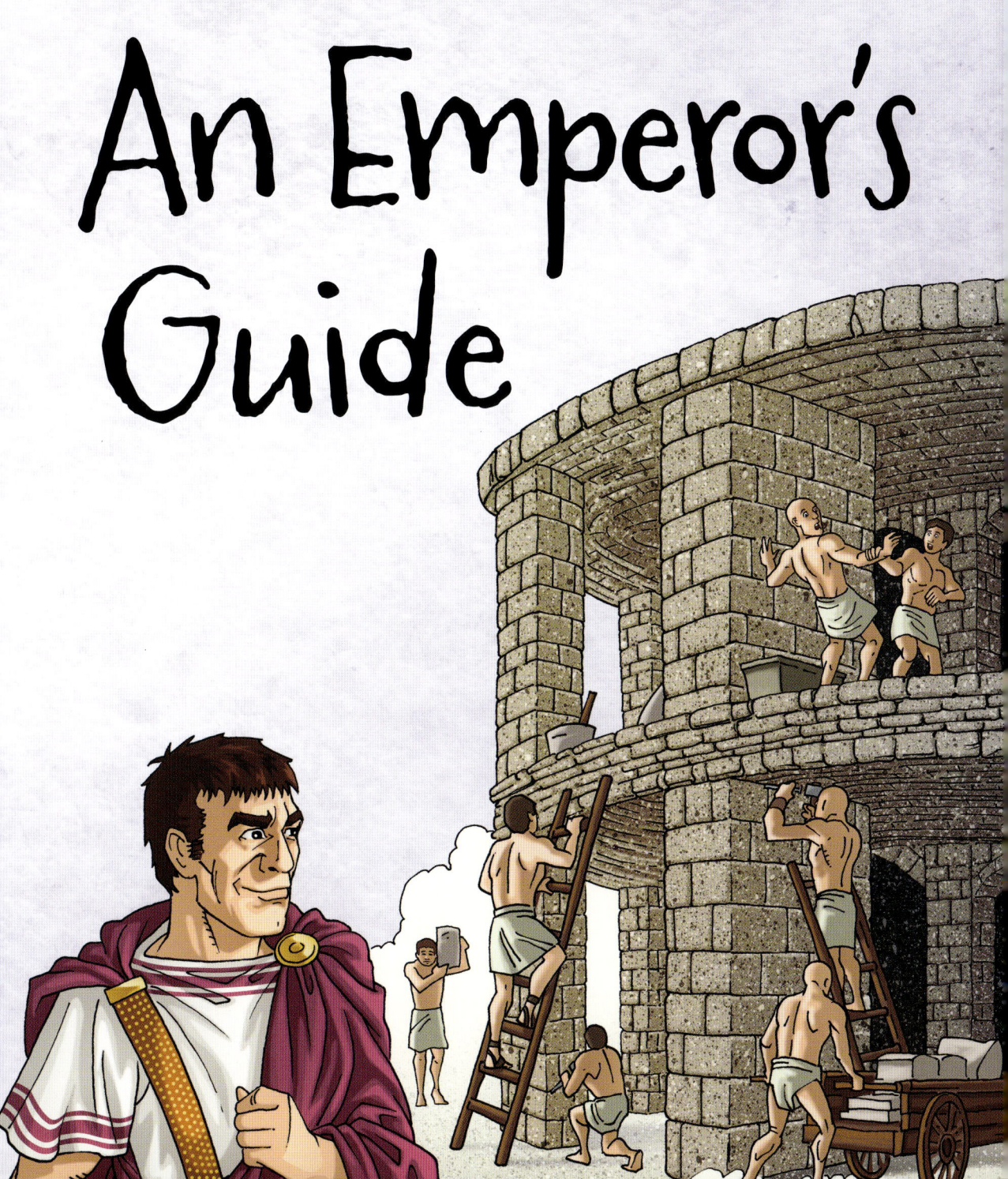

Thanks to the creative team:
Senior Editor: Alice Peebles
Consultant: John Haywood
Fact Checker: Kate Mitchell
Design: www.collaborate.agency

Original edition copyright 2016 by Hungry Tomato Ltd.
Copyright © 2017 by Lerner Publishing Group, Inc.
Hungry Tomato™ is a trademark of Lerner Publishing Group, Inc.

All rights reserved. International copyright secured. No part of this book may be reproduced, stored in a retrieval system, or transmitted in any form or by any means—electronic, mechanical, photocopying, recording, or otherwise—without the prior written permission of Lerner Publishing Group, Inc., except for the inclusion of brief quotations in an acknowledged review.

Hungry Tomato™
A division of Lerner Publishing Group, Inc.
241 First Avenue North
Minneapolis, MN 55401 USA
For reading levels and more information, look up this title at www.lernerbooks.com.

Main body text set in Blokletters Balpen 9/13.
Typeface provided by LeFly Fonts.

Library of Congress Cataloging-in-Publication Data

The Cataloging-in-Publication Data for *An Emperor's Guide* is on file at the Library of Congress.
978-1-5124-1551-3 (lib. bdg.)
978-1-5124-3071-4 (pbk.)
978-1-5124-2707-3 (EB pdf)

Manufactured in the United States of America
1-39911-21381-8/10/2016

How-To Guides for Fiendish Rulers

An Emperor's Guide

by Catherine Chambers
Illustrated by Ryan Pentney

CONTENTS

Writing Down My Rules	6
How I Became Emperor	8
Ruling in this Life and the Next	10
Everyone in their Place . . .	12
Power to the People? Not Likely	14
Protecting My Position	16
My Lavish Lifestyle	18
Building My Capital	20
Being a Bad Neighbor	22
I Order You to Have Fun	24
My Powerful Death	26
Gods and Goddesses	28
Ten More Fiendish Emperors	30
Index	32

Writing Down My Rules

I am a Roman emperor and have ruled my vast empire for many years. **MY SUBJECTS MUST OBEY ME.** After all, I give them bread to eat. I entertain them in my circuses too. I am very wise to keep them happy. But I am also a bit old. So I need to teach my son all my rules before he becomes Emperor. My scribes are writing them down carefully.

MY RULES MUST BE WRITTEN CLEARLY. My scribes begin, using the best papyrus paper and ink. I can hear their reed pens scratching away. My chief scribe watches over them. I do not want any hidden jokes or ink blots.

I am now lying down to ease my aches and pains. I feel death just around the corner. The scribes must work quickly. I call for a priest. He wrings his hands at the thought of my death. He takes some fine food to the altar of the Parcae, the Fates who decide when we die. The priest asks him how long I have got. There is no reply. I feel sick with worry.

My trusted consul, a top official, now fetches the royal doctor. He is from Greece, like many doctors here in Rome. My last doctor prescribed unwashed wool for a sore eye, and I stank all day. So I banished him to far-off Britain.

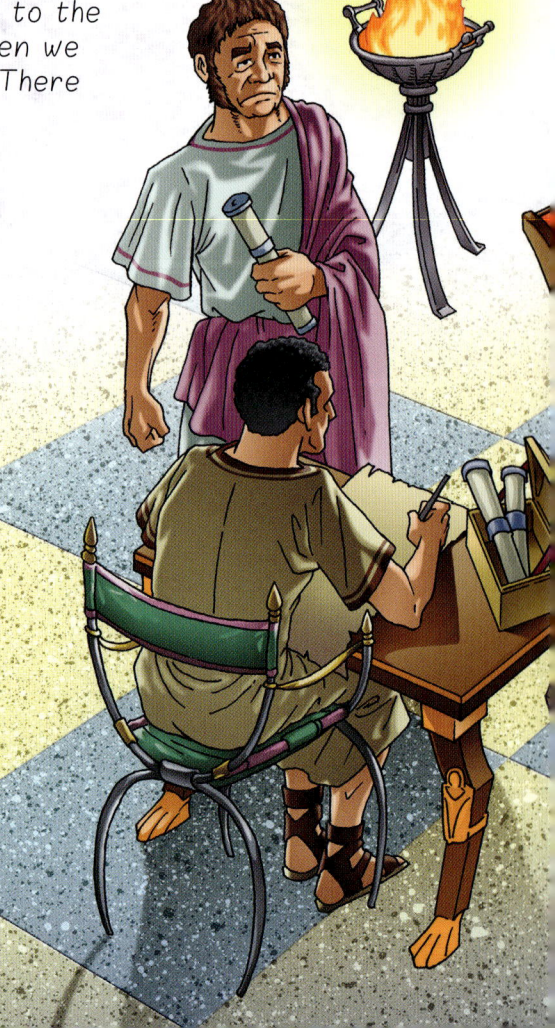

My new doctor tells me that my four humors are unbalanced. These humors are black bile, which is vomit; yellow bile, which is diarrhea; blood; and phlegm, or spit. The doctor advises me to eat less fat and do more exercise. I should drink herbal medicine to upset my stomach, and he offers to scorch my skin with a hot iron. I simply refuse to eat less fat and do more exercise. Is he trying to kill me?

The scribes have laid down their pens. They are blowing the ink dry on my final words. The rules are clear. My work is done. I know my son will thank me for these rules. I hope you do too. OR ELSE!

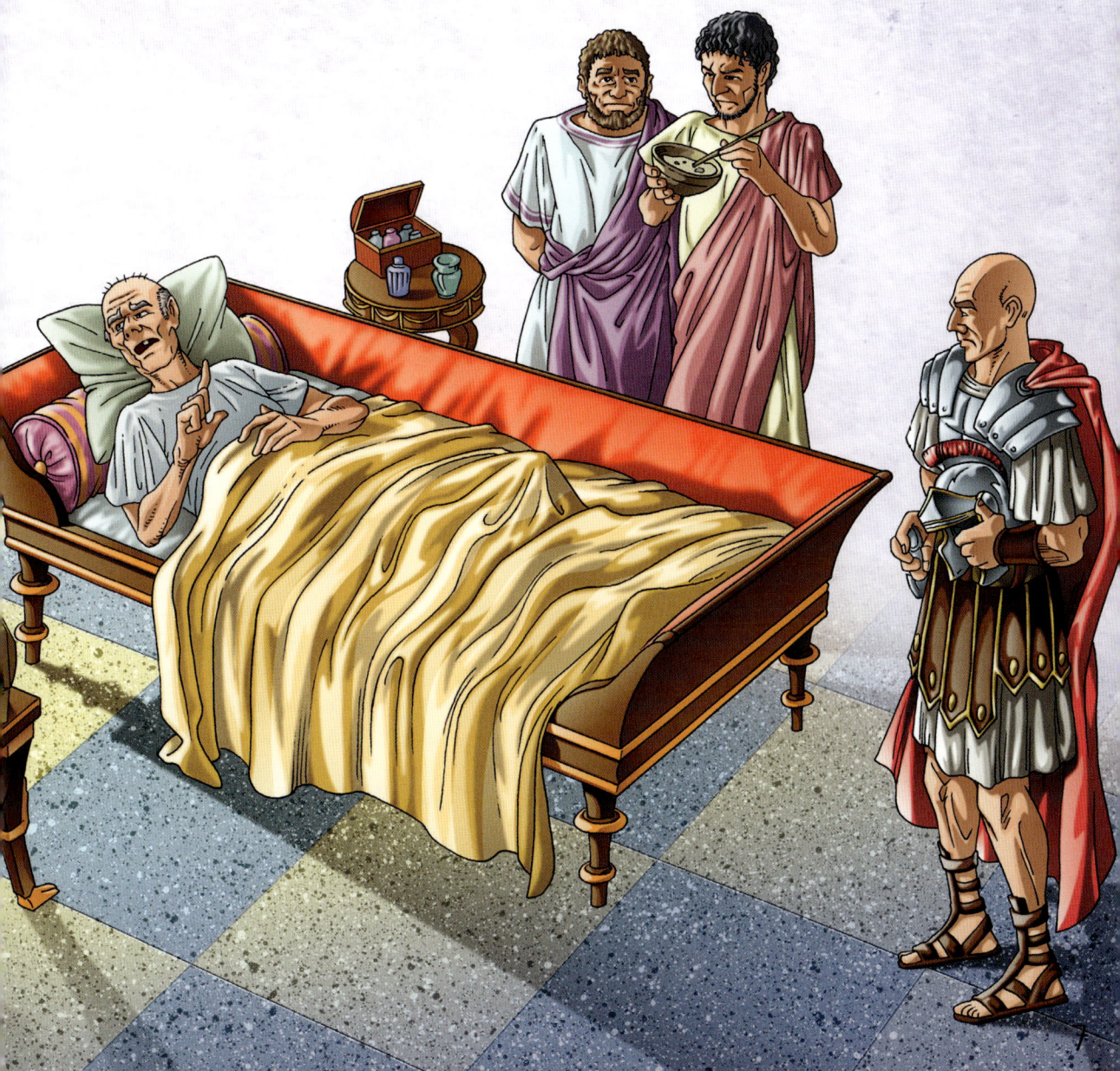

How I Became Emperor

It is my absolute right to be Emperor of Rome and all the lands under my rule, from the Mediterranean to northern Europe. I inherited the position from my father. My son will become Emperor when I'm dead, unless scheming nobles intervene. If they kill my son before I die, I might train a nephew or an adopted son to take over.

I think I need just a little bit more . . .

RESPECT MY KNOWLEDGE!

An emperor does not need to be well-educated. But my knowledge of mathematics, literature, and history helps me win arguments with my consuls. My wife has also studied though girls cannot go to school. She was educated in her home by a tutor, who was a slave. How gracious I am to allow some slaves to improve their lives. Anyway, you can see that our son is the child of very smart parents. He'll make a great Emperor.

You must understand that I WILL NOT TOLERATE TRAITORS. It is unbelievable how nobles and generals plot to overthrow me. Sometimes they even try to assassinate me! At other times, noble families quarrel and fight among themselves. This makes Rome an unstable and dangerous place for me. A great noble general could easily rise from the chaos and take over.

IT IS MY RIGHT TO BANISH YOU. If I feel that people are plotting against my son or me, I banish them to the far corners of my Empire. I especially like sending them to Britain, where it is cold, wet, and unfriendly. There are no opportunities for networking, so their schemes die. Hopefully the barbarians will make sure that they die too.

Fiendish Fact File

- The Roman Empire took over from the Republic of Rome (509–27 BCE). The Republic was a democracy, so elected, wealthy magistrates made the decisions and laws.

- Julius Caesar (ruled 46–44 BCE) declared himself dictator for life. This marked the end of the Republic and the beginning of the Empire. Caesar was assassinated by senators who wanted to restore the Republic. His nephew and adopted son, Octavian, fought his way through civil wars to become the first emperor, Augustus.

Ruling in this Life and the Next

I expect my subjects to treat me as a god. I certainly behave like one. Of course I am not exactly a god, but I hope to become one when I die. Meanwhile, my subjects across the Empire should build altars and temples in my name. They must make offerings and sacrifices too. Hopefully coins stamped with my gorgeous face will remind them how wonderful I am. So will the hundreds of statues that I have displayed all over the Empire.

Just a little more on the cheekbones. Less on the nose.

I INSIST ON BECOMING A GOD. I ask my senators if they will make me a god when I die. I ask my son too. None of them give me a straight answer. I have a chance if I am not too cruel and give my people enough bread. Then a coin will be made with my head stamped on it. I am drawing up the designs now with my imperial sculptor.

I AM THE CHIEF PRIEST! Even the augurs, or priests from the colleges, listen to me—mostly. They are elected for life, so murder is the only way of getting rid of them. They can read signs from the gods, both good and bad. I make sure my people hear only good news. They must believe the gods are on my side.

I hope it's a message from Bacchus, the god of parties.

MY SUBJECTS MUST HONOR GODS AT FESTIVALS. This is not hard as they get a day off work. In December it is Saturnalia, the festival for the seed god, Saturn. Then my subjects take nearly a week off! They dance along the streets and exchange gifts. I even pay for them to eat meat at public feasts. For the whole week, masters wait on their slaves. I become very popular at this time because I allow the masses to say exactly what they think!

I WILL NOT PUT UP WITH UNGODLY RIOTS. On March 19 I allow a festival for the goddess Minerva. She looks after all the craftsmen and protects wise people like me. On Minerva Day there are a lot of carpenters and stonemasons running around the streets. I'll make sure there is a good supply of bread to keep them all happy. No bread means hungry people and no peace!

Fiendish Fact File

- Augurs made predictions based on the shapes of the livers taken from animals that had been sacrificed.

- April 25 was the feast of Robigalia, the god of rust disease on wheat. He was honored through the sacrifice of a rust-colored dog and a sheep.

Everyone in their Place...

Senators advise me while mighty magistrates judge lawbreakers. But I have the final say over all these noble people. They are lucky to serve the Empire, so I do not pay them a single *denarius*. A noble must own property worth at least one million *sesterces* before he becomes a senator. Rich is good. Then they won't need to steal from me.

I'm broke! I put all my money in property.

I HAVE GREAT EXPECTATIONS FOR MY NOBLES.
Most of them are sons of nobles, but this does not mean they can sit back. A young noble has to study law, practice it, and get rich at the same time. He must join the army and become a distinguished officer too. If he has enough breath left, he should learn oration. That means he has to speak in public about anything from poetry to politics.

YOU MUST WORK HARD!
A hard-working noble will become a senator or even a consul in my senate. After a few years, I will let him retire! My rules allow him to become a governor of a province, which I will choose for him. There he will get lots of tribute from all the poor citizens and become very rich indeed. My rules can be so kind.

This feels like the middle of nowhere! Why ME?

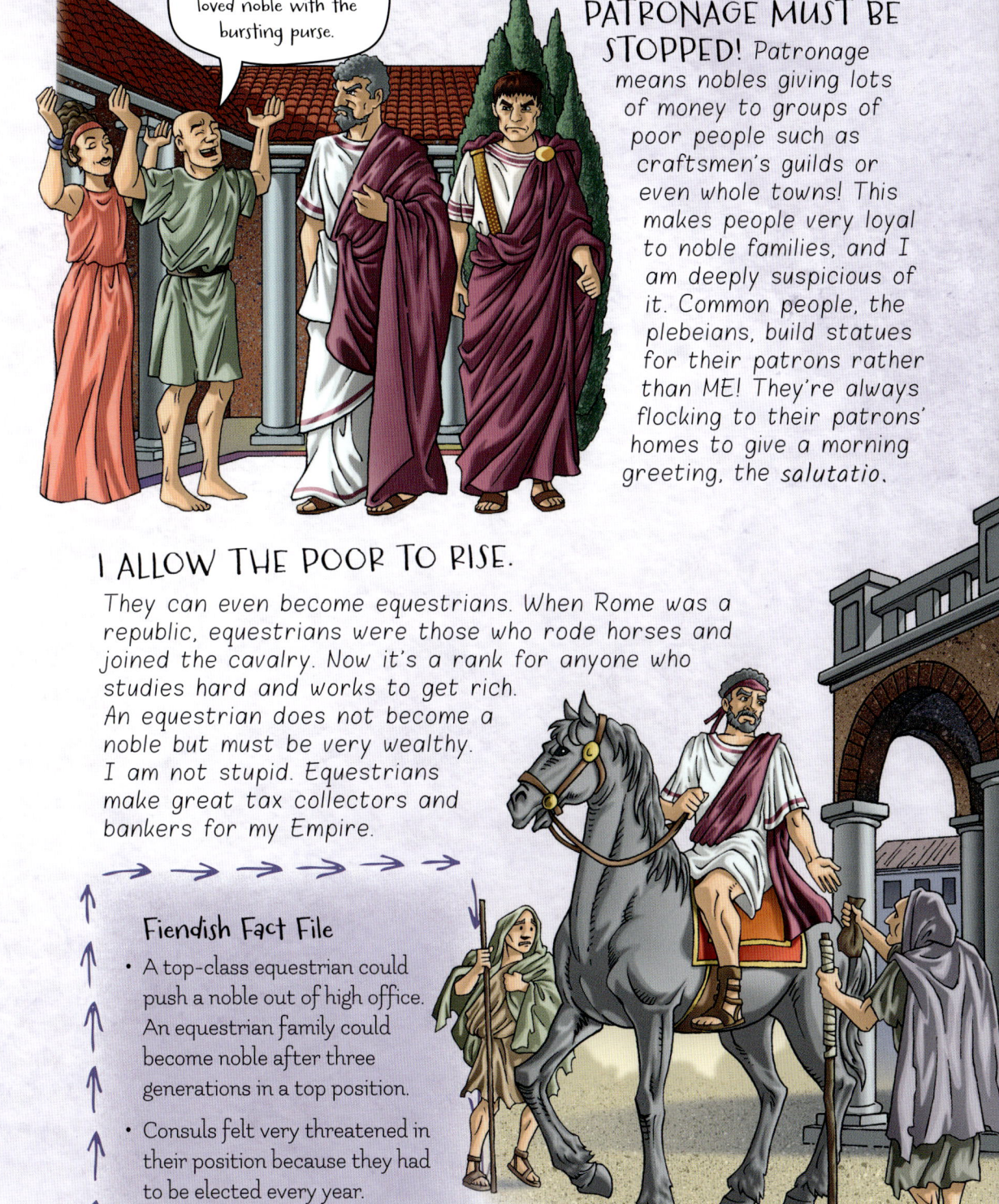

Power to the People? Not Likely

Naturally, I make the rules for the lowly plebeians, or plebs. Long ago, these ordinary citizens could call an assembly to get laws passed. But I don't allow it anymore. Their true place is near the bottom of the pile where they can look down on freedmen and, of course, slaves. Slaves are usually foreign captives, and I don't care about them.

- Consuls and senators
- Nobles and wealthy plebeians (working people)
- Plebeians (artisans, craftspeople)
- Freedmen
- Slaves

I DO NOT ALLOW MOBS!

Working people such as craftsmen, builders, and farmers are strong and unruly. They like to riot—over anything. So I allow them just a little freedom of speech. They can form workers' groups, take part in meetings, and elect officials. I know exactly what goes on because I send in my spies.

Which one of us is the spy?

A MAN CANNOT USE HIS WIFE TO RISE ABOVE HIS STATION.

That means you cannot sneak into the class above you by marrying someone of higher status. And remember: your children will take on the class of your wife. So make sure she's not too lowly. I am rather afraid of middle- and upper-class women. They may become patrons of the poor. That's way too powerful.

A POPULAR EMPEROR HELPS THE POOR.

I am so generous to the plebs of Rome and the poor peasant migrants who come looking for work here. I give them bread, grain, olive oil, and wine. I even hand out cash to celebrate military victories. Lots of them can get jobs on my building projects. Free tickets to the theater and hippodrome help them to relax. And the public baths are so cheap! They love me!

IF YOU ARE A HARDWORKING AND OBEDIENT SLAVE, I MIGHT SET YOU FREE!

Some slaves, especially those who live in the city, can buy their own freedom. They are still not citizens and cannot hold political positions, but their children can. These freedmen and women need all the correct paperwork to cut ties with their owners. A magistrate then grants them total freedom, or manumission. Don't worry about the owners. There are always plenty more slaves.

Fiendish Fact File

- Emperor Augustus (ruled 27 BCE–14 CE) stopped the plebeians from making laws. He ended the power of the tribunes who represented them.

- Slaves working in mines and quarries were treated cruelly. Escaped slaves who were recaptured had to wear an iron collar showing their owner's name.

- Public welfare for poor plebeians was established by Emperor Titus (ruled 79-81 CE) and Emperor Trajan (ruled 98-117 CE).

Protecting My Position

My Praetorian Guards protect my body but cannot save me from spies. I am always under threat from scheming noble enemies—and so called friends. One of my best rules is to build private rooms in my palaces so that no one can overhear me. Unfortunately my nobles do that too. So it is hard for my spies to hear what they are saying about ME.

What luck! He reads out loud.

They're talking about their holidays—it could be a secret code ...

I WATCH OUT FOR MY SENATORS. They hate me because they, not emperors, used to run Rome. They all have their own spy network. Mostly, Roman nobles spy on each other, but sometimes they focus on ME! They use business networks and even slaves as spies. So do I! Sometimes I find out that one of my sneaky enemies has done something shocking. Then I can create a public scandal and push him out of the way.

I SEND SPIES ONTO THE STREETS. Street sellers chatting and greeting passersby look so innocent. But trust me, they're not! They know everything that's going on. That's why I send my *frumentarii* officials into the crowds. Frumentarii once bought and gave out grain over a wide area. So they heard all the gossip. Now they work with the urban police for ME and listen to the word on the street.

I KEEP AN EYE ON TRAITORS ACROSS THE EMPIRE. Even my generals fighting in far-off lands try to get rid of me, in spite of all the land I give them. So I use couriers, called *speculatores*, to spy on them and bring me documents detailing their treachery. Speculatores are very useful. They arrest political rivals, guard suspects, and execute guilty traitors.

Fiendish Fact File

- The Praetorian Guard was always paid well. But it did not stop them from murdering emperors, such as Elagabalus (ruled 218-222 CE). His cousin, Alexander Severus (ruled 222-235 CE), was installed in his place.

- Frumentarii also spied on armies and by the third century CE were raiding villages and asking locals for bribes.

- Emperor Diocletian (ruled 284-305 CE) disbanded the corrupt frumentarii and installed the *agentes in rebus*, or general agents. They became just as treacherous.

YOU WILL MARRY THIS NOBLE TO MAKE HIM LOYAL TO ME!

I try to make friends with my nobles by offering my sisters, daughters, and nieces as their brides. This helps to create alliances though sometimes the nobles divorce these lovely women. Then I'm in trouble.

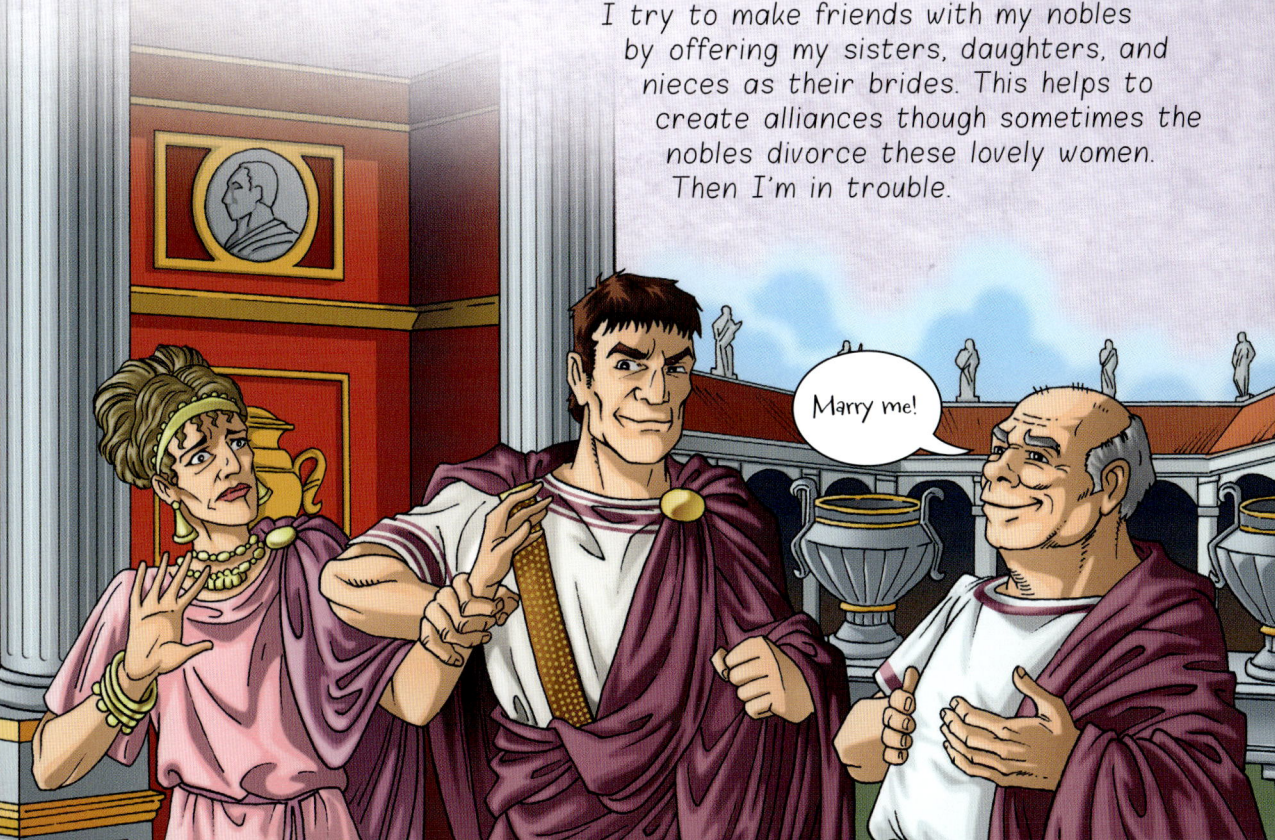

Marry me!

My Lavish Lifestyle

Life at the top is expensive and luxurious. That is my rule. My clothes stand out so that people across the Empire will recognize me. Today, my toga is of fine purple silk edged with gold. Soft, colored leather sandals cover my feet. My head is crowned with laurel leaves when I go out. I am about to perfom my duties as high priest. A slave will pull the toga over my head like a hood.

I need to see the rank of every citizen, so **EACH SOCIAL CLASS WILL WEAR WHAT I SAY!** My senators can be recognized by their expensive linen togas. These have wide purple stripes while the equestrians below them wear narrow purple stripes. But I will punish anyone who wears too much royal purple! Ordinary working citizens and many slaves need only short, coarse woollen togas. But I am full of surprises. Sometimes I give gold jewelry to my favorite palace slaves.

Mind my hair!

I CANNOT MAKE RULES ON AN EMPTY STOMACH.

I just love eating, but I eat only the most expensive, exotic foods. Flamingo tongues are a real favorite, though peacock brains come close. I insist on many courses for my banquets, with spectacular displays. My finest chefs must delight guests with strange but edible beasts such as rabbits with duck wings attached. Ice cream finishes the meal off nicely. I actually love smoked cheese, but I keep that quiet. Even soldiers can afford it. A few lettuce leaves after an evening meal help me to sleep.

The cheese is under the grapes.

FREE WHEAT FOR THE WORKERS!

I make sure that the plebs have enough bread to eat—it keeps them from rioting. Most of them live in tiny high-rise apartments where a smoky oven would be a problem. But they can always take their loaves to the baker's shop. On the way, these simple people buy takeout sausages and fried fish. It is a lie that they can only afford bread, porridge, lentils, and vegetable soup!

This urine is so strong it's burning the cloth!

Fiendish Fact File

- Clothes were taken to wash houses where workers called fullers cleaned them. Fullers used sulphur and human urine to remove the dirt.
- When the weather was chilly, Romans put on extra tunics. Most wore three. But Emperor Augustus hated the cold, so he wore four.
- Citizens' teeth were ground down by grit and coarse grains in their bread flour.

Building My Capital

I love Rome. I make sure its massive gleaming buildings show my power and wealth. There is nothing finer than entering the towering Colosseum or the Forum with its grand triumphal arches.

I DO NOT PAY FOR ROME. Every time I conquer new lands, I get more people to pay taxes. This means I have extra money to spend on building my capital. Of course, I get more slaves too. They do all the hard work on my building sites and in my limestone and marble quarries.

I MUST FOLLOW THE EXAMPLE OF MY HERO.

Emperor Augustus said, "I found Rome built of sun-dried bricks; I leave her clothed in marble." So I shall continue to build palaces, temples, arenas, theaters, baths, aqueducts, and bridges on a grand scale. My most important employees are my engineers. They design strong arches that hold up most of these structures.

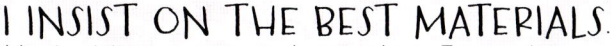

I INSIST ON THE BEST MATERIALS.

My buildings are so huge that I need very tough materials such as travertine limestone. A strong mortar holds the stone and brickwork together. My master builders mix lime and rubble with volcanic ash called *pozzolana*, dug up in Naples—a busy but rather lowly city.

THERE IS NO EXCUSE FOR AN UGLY BUILDING.

I like my brickwork to be laid in pleasing patterns. Bare stone walls should shine with a thin layer of beautiful marble. As for my baths, they are decorated with mosaics made from small marble and glass tesserae. I like blue and green best. They make my baths look like the sea. Many mosaic scenes are of water gods, sea creatures, and waves. My nobles decorate their villas almost as well as my palaces, which is very annoying.

Fiendish Fact File

- After the Fall of Rome, the great Forum fell apart. For centuries it was called the Campo Vaccino, or Cow Field, because a cattle market was held there.

- Buildings and bathhouses were heated with warm air that circulated under floors and between walls. Slave labor stoked the underground furnaces.

- Emperor Augustus built his Great Palace on the Palatine Hill, which gives us the word palace.

Being a Bad Neighbor

I need a huge empire so I can gather lots of taxes from conquered peoples. One of my main rules is to take land that is good for growing grain. A lot of grain makes Romans happy. My diplomats try to ask foreign rulers politely for tribute and access to their mines and trade routes. If they refuse, then I send in the troops! A loyal legion of six thousand fighters should do the trick. Let's hope they bring back a lot of defeated slaves.

I MUST KEEP SOLDIERS HAPPY! I pay my lucky soldiers *denarii* to fight for me. When I first became Emperor, I gave my soldiers a donative. This special payment made them very happy indeed. I give my legions a pension when they retire and allow them to marry. Some even take home bronze, silver, or gold disks or armbands that they have won in battle.

I INSIST ON THE BEST WEAPONS. I command the most senior camp prefect, the *praefectus castrorum,* to sort out all the equipment. He's in charge of grueling training too. My wealthy and powerful centurions get the finest iron-tipped javelins, razor-sharp *gladii* (short swords), bronze shields, and helmets. The lower ranks of simple foot soldiers only need slings. They are very easily replaced with reservists when they are killed.

It's tough at the top. **I EXPECT HIGH STANDARDS FROM MY OFFICERS, THE CENTURIONS.** I detest any brutality—unless I've ordered it. A quick-tempered young officer shows lack of discipline. He will NEVER become a senator. An officer must show bravery and skill and NOT mind getting wet, cold, and dirty like his soldiers. Being friendly and soft could destroy my Empire. So when a centurion fights in a foreign land, he should avoid picking up local customs.

Never mind the enemy. How about that juicy rabbit for lunch?

I only signed up because I wanted to travel.

Fiendish Fact File

- Early Roman legions came from local regions around Rome. Citizens performed military service as a duty so were not paid and had to provide their own weapons!

- Rome's Publius Cornelius Scipio (died 211 BCE) was defeated in Italy by Hannibal and his elephants from North Africa. This led to better battle tactics rather than brute force.

- The Emperor took all the credit for his generals' victories. This stopped Romans from supporting a successful general instead of their Emperor.

23

I Order You to Have Fun

It might be free, but you still need a valid ticket!

Mostly I rule with a rod of iron. However I realize it is good sense to keep the plebeians happy. So I organize free entertainment on a grand scale in my arenas and amphitheaters. The Circus Maximus and the Colosseum are my favorite venues, and they show my wealth and power.

I GET THE BEST SEAT! I am very proud of my concrete Colosseum. It houses the best and bloodiest entertainment. All the seats are marble. But the unwashed plebeians must sit on a plank of wood in the top rows. Those ranked above them may use a *curule*, a nice, soft cushion. As for me, I have the best view from the Imperial boxes at the north and south ends. I allow my senators to bring chairs.

MY RULES IN THE RING. First, expensive dramas take place on stage with scenery made from real trees. Lions occasionally provide some violence, which is quickly followed by amazing circus acrobats. Then the real crowd-pleasers arrive: the gladiators! I sometimes allow the common people to decide their fate. After the bodies have been cleared away, Rome's best orators recite poems, mostly praising me. Though some say they contain hidden meanings. How ungrateful!

See how our great leader loves his people...

Hooray!

BRING ON MY FAVORITE GLADIATOR! Two gladiators from the four different fighting classes enter the ring. Their manager, the *lanista*, is close at hand. He's ready to prod them with a hot iron if they're slow. My command is obeyed, and my favorite gladiator from the *Retiarius* class appears. He wears no armor or helmet, only a shoulder pad. He throws a net over his armored opponent and lunges at him with his pointed trident. Hooray! Oh, he missed.

Fiendish Fact File
- The lanista (which means butcher) was often cruel when coaching his gladiators.
- The most successful charioteer was Scorpus, who won two thousand races.
- Fans of rival chariot teams wrote curses on stone tablets to upset the opposition.

WHEN I CHEER FOR A CHARIOT, SO MUST YOU! In the Circus Maximus, 250,000 spectators roar as I cheer on the most famous charioteer. Up to twelve chariots speed around the track. Drivers try to hold on, but some are tossed off their lightweight carriages, trampled by horses, or caught in the reins. Shame. After, my lucky subjects go shopping in the mall around the arena.

My Powerful Death

My death might be dramatic, so I insist on a funeral to match. That means a procession with a lot of wailing and solemn music. Of course I will be buried within Rome's city walls along with the upper classes. The rest of my subjects will be buried outside. I do not approve of social mixing, even underground.

YOU WILL MOURN FOR ME—OR ELSE! My beautifully dressed body will be carried in an expensive coffin set on a stand. Hundreds of expensive professional mourners will wail, pull their hair out, and claw their skin until the blood runs. I insist on a large orchestra of flute players. I also expect a great monument to be built in my honor. I'm actually working on that now.

RULES FOR UPPER-CLASS FUNERALS. I wish I could change these rules, but they are very ancient, so I don't dare. Dead consuls are dressed in gowns edged in royal purple. Even better, military heroes wear vests embroidered with gold thread. Their noble bodies are paraded upright through the streets in chariots until they reach the great arched Forum. Here, they are set on an expensive ivory chair. Spoiled in life and in death.

I ALLOW NOBLES TO KEEP THEIR ANCESTORS IN A CUPBOARD.

Not real ancestors, just their wax funeral masks, called *imagines*. Some families keep imagines that go back many generations. They show the nobles' power and make me really nervous. At funerals, all the masks come out of the wooden cupboard. They are then lavishly decorated and worn by actors during the procession.

ALL YOU POOR PEOPLE WILL BECOME LOWLY SPIRITS.

We call these inferior spirits shades—very dull. Your souls will be carried by boat across the River Styx, between Earth and Hades, or hell. Then you will face Pluto, the god of the Underworld.

Fiendish Fact File
- Romans believed that shade spirits could get very angry if unkind things were said about them. Then they could get revenge on the gossips.
- Early Roman emperors were cremated, and their ashes were placed in an expensive urn.

And if no one makes offerings or says nice things about you, your spirit will float around with no memory. But I don't care. I will become a god. Long live ME!

Gods and Goddesses

Here are some of my favorite gods and goddesses. We adopted most of them from the Greeks and changed their names, and sometimes their stories.

SATURN is the god of agriculture, freedom, plenty, and time. We celebrate him at a very jolly festival called Saturnalia.

JUPITER is Saturn's son. He fiendishly took over as king of all gods. He is also the god of the sky, thunder, and bolts of lightning. My generals visit his temples with expensive offerings.

JUNO protects women and is important, like Jupiter. Some say she is his wife. Juno became very jealous of the goddess Minerva, who was born from the top of Jupiter's head.

MARS is Juno's son and was once the god of farming. He is now the god of war and the protector of Rome. We celebrate him every March, which is named after him.

NEPTUNE is Jupiter's brother and the god of the sea. His festival is on July 23, a month when water is scarce. So we want to please him to bring rain.

PENATES protect the home and Rome. Each household has a shrine to them and gives them a portion of their meals. I give cakes and honey—or blood.

PLUTO is god of the Underworld and judge of the dead, often shown with a three-headed dog. He gave us gold and silver from the Earth, so he was linked with the Underworld.

VULCAN is the destructive god of fire. We build his temples outside Rome for safety. At his festival, Volcanalia, on August 23, noblemen throw small, tasty fish into a fire.

Ten More Fiendish Emperors

Some of these Roman emperors ruled without being fiendish at all—but others were fiendish indeed!

1. Julius Caesar (dictator 46–44 BCE) turned Rome from a Republic, with elected senators, into an Empire. He conquered many lands but did not kill his captives or take their property. He declared himself dictator and was murdered by senators.

2. Augustus (ruled 43 BCE–14 CE) was Julius Caesar's great nephew and Rome's first true Emperor. He created a regular army, constructed impressive buildings, and loved poetry. He then lost a lot of territory, which made him harsh.

3. Tiberius (ruled 14–37 CE) was successful in battle and improved Rome's finances and administration. But he poisoned his adopted son and successor, Germanicus.

4. Caligula (ruled 37–41 CE) was the son of Germanicus. He fell ill in 37 CE, after which he became cruel and irrational. Among his crimes were the murder of his closest supporter and best friend, Macro. His citizens were executed for saying the word goat in front of him (he took it personally as he had a hairy body).

5. Nero (ruled 54–68 CE) at first listened to his advisers, Seneca and Burrus, but Burrus died, and Seneca retired. Nero killed both his mother and his daughter, and Rome went up in flames.

6 Trajan (ruled 98–117 CE) expanded the Roman Empire eastward to Dacia (now Romania), Armenia, and Arabia. He lowered taxes and helped poor children.

7 Hadrian (ruled 117–138 CE) was governor of Syria and was in charge of the Persian Parthian Wars. He abandoned both as Emperor. He built great structures such as Hadrian's Wall in Britain and pleased Romans with gruesome gladiatorial spectacles.

8 Septimius Severus (ruled 193–211 CE) was always fighting wars and plotting against rival generals. When one of them, Clodius Albinus, died in battle against him, Severus cut off his head and sent it to Rome. He also executed many senators.

9 Diocletian (ruled 284–305 CE) possibly had two emperors murdered while he was the head of the Imperial Bodyguard. A fiendish start, which he continued by persecuting Christians mercilessly. He spent Rome's money on a glittering bathhouse in Rome and a retirement palace in Croatia.

10 Romulus Augustulus (ruled 475–476 CE), the last Emperor, who ruled briefly as a teenager, was named after Romulus, the first heroic king of Rome. Augustulus means "the little Augustus"— after the first Emperor. Romulus Augustulus lost the Empire and retired with lots of money to a palace.

INDEX

Augustus, Emperor, 9, 15, 19, 21, 30

becoming an emperor, 8-9
buildings, 20-21, 30

Caligula, Emperor, 30
centurions, 23
chariots, 25-26
clothes, 18-19

Diocletian, Emperor, 17, 31
doctors, 6-7

entertainment, 24-25
equestrians, 13, 18

festivals, 11, 28-29
food, 18-19
funerals, 26-27

gladiators, 25, 31
gods and goddesses, 10-11, 27-29

Hadrian, Emperor, 31

Julius Caesar, 9, 30
Juno, 28
Jupiter, 28-29

Mars, 28
Minerva, 11, 28

Neptune, 29
Nero, Emperor, 30
nobles, 8-9, 12-13, 16-17, 21, 26-27, 29

patronage, 13, 15
Pluto, 27, 29
Praetorian Guards, 16-17
priests, 6, 10, 18

Saturn, 11, 28
senators, 9-10, 12, 16, 18, 23-24, 30-31
slaves, 8, 11, 14-16, 18, 20-22
social class, 13-15, 18-19, 25-26
soldiers, 18, 22-23
spies, 14, 16-17

Tiberius, Emperor, 30
traitors, 9, 17
Trajan, Emperor, 15, 31

Vulcan, 29

weapons, 23

The Author
Catherine Chambers was born in Adelaide, South Australia and brought up in England. She earned a degree in African History and Swahili at the School of Oriental and African Studies, London. Catherine has written around 130 titles for children and young adults, mainly non-fiction, and she enjoys seeking out intriguing facts for her non-fiction titles.

The Illustrator
Ryan Pentney lives and works in Norwich in the United Kingdom. Growing up in the 1990s, he was surrounded by iconic cartoons, comics, and books that have remained a passion with him. Inspired by these childhood heroes as well as more modern works, Ryan creates his own characters and stories in the hope of inspiring the next generation. He uses the latest technology and traditional techniques to make stylized digital artworks.